Fish

by Molly Bridger

Printed in the United States of America

ISBN 0-15-313907-2

Ordering Options
ISBN 0-15-314004-6 (Grade 4 Collection)
ISBN 0-15-314116-6 (package of 5)

2 3 4 5 6 7 8 9 10 026 99

"Japan!" Luke exclaimed. "We have to go to Japan?"

"We'll have a wonderful time," Mom said.

"It's only for six months," Dad said.

Six months. Luke looked around his bedroom. He loved this room. He loved his books and his baseball card collection. He looked at his goldfish. He thought about the kids in his class and on his baseball team.

"I can't leave!" Luke said. "What about baseball? What about Swish and Fin and all my friends?"

"You can bring your baseball cards along," Dad said, "But your fish and your friends will have to stay here."

"You'll make new friends," Mom said. "It will be great fun."

1

But it wasn't fun. It wasn't fun at all. In Japan, Luke's mom and dad worked most of the time. He went to school.

School was okay. At least people there spoke English. But it was the middle of the year. Everyone else had already made friends.

The other kids came from all over the world. No one played baseball. The school was big and spread out. They went to different rooms for each class. Luke kept getting lost.

"The school rambles all over the place," he complained to his mother. "I'm always late to class."

"Ask a friend for help," his mom replied.

Luke didn't have a friend. He felt abandoned.

At first, Luke spent a lot of time in his new bedroom.

It was different from his room at home. The floor had mats made out of straw. His bed, called a futon, was like a mattress on the floor.

Luke had space to sort baseball cards. Without a friend, though, baseball cards weren't much fun.

Every afternoon after school, Luke threw himself on his futon and dreamed about home. He missed his best friend, Mark. He missed his goldfish, too. Without Swish and Fin, he didn't have anyone to complain to.

After a while, staying in his room got boring. Even though he didn't know how to talk to people, Luke went for long walks around his new town.

There was so much to see. The signs were in a different language, with different letters. People wore different kinds of shoes on their feet. Even the dogs looked different. Luke couldn't recognize many of the breeds.

He passed people who smiled at him. Some even talked to him, but he couldn't understand what they said.

Once he bumped into a lady. She smiled and she looked so kind!

Luke said, "Excuse me."

To himself, he pretended that she was his first new friend. Maybe she was the wife of the most famous baseball player in Japan. She would introduce them, and they would go to all the games.

But the lady just bowed and said something Luke could not understand. She was just one of many passersby.

"I wish I had somebody to talk to," Luke said out loud. Nobody answered.

One day, Luke found a small park near his
house. It had benches and paths. It also had a pool,
and the pool was full of fish.

Luke sat down on a bench by the pool.

"Hi," he said to the fish.

The fish didn't say anything back. But Luke felt
they were listening to him, just like Fin and Swish.

"You remind me of my fish at home," he said.

The fish glided around in the pool. One swam to
the top of the water. It opened its mouth. Then it
dove down again.

"Swish and Fin do that, too," Luke told the fish. "I miss them. Mark is taking care of them for me."

The fish swam close to the edge of the pool.

"I miss Mark," Luke said. "I miss my whole fourth grade class." He leaned over the pool.

"Do you know I can't even get my favorite ice cream here? The other day, Dad bought me some ice cream. He thought it was chocolate. I like chocolate best. But it wasn't chocolate. It was bean paste. Bean paste ice cream!"

The fish swam around calmly.

7

"I'm sure bean paste ice cream is very good, if that is what you expect." Luke sighed.

He thought about other things he missed.

"I miss all my friends. I miss crawling under my bed and looking for lost socks. I miss sticking posters on my wall. But most of all, aside from friends, I miss baseball. . ."

"*Beisu boru?*"

Luke looked up. A boy was sitting on the other end of the bench. He had a baseball hat on his head. He was holding a baseball glove and a bat. He was holding a paper bag, too.

"Baseball!" Luke said. "Do you play?" He point-ed at the boy, then swung a pretend bat to make sure he understood.

The boy nodded his head.

"*Beisu boru*," he repeated. He pointed to the far side of the park.

Luke looked. He saw lots of kids over there. Some were tossing balls back and forth. A couple were swinging bats. A few were stretching.

The boy pointed at them. Then he pointed at Luke. He spoke so quickly that Luke couldn't tell where one word ended and the next one began. But Luke didn't need a translation. The boy wanted Luke to play, too.

"I don't have a glove," Luke said, holding up his bare hand.

The boy replied. Even though he spoke in Japanese, Luke knew what he meant. He could borrow a glove.

"Okay! I'm ready," Luke said, jumping off the bench. "Let's go!"

But first the boy held up the paper bag. He took a pinch of stuff from inside and sprinkled it in the pond. The fish gulped it up.

Then the boy offered the bag to Luke.

Luke couldn't believe it. His new friend liked baseball *and* fish. Maybe he liked baseball cards, too.

"Thank you," Luke said as he took the bag. He scattered more food on the pond for the fish. As he did it, he whispered thank you to the fish, too.

Then, while the fish gobbled up their snack, Luke and his new companion went off to play base-ball together.

Try This!

Here are some Japanese words that Luke's new friend might teach him. Try saying them aloud.

ichi	[ee´chi]	=	one
ni	[nee]	=	two
san	[sahn]	=	three
hi	[hee]	=	day/sun
getsu	[get´soo]	=	month/moon
yama	[yah´mah]	=	mountain
kawa	[kah´wah]	=	river
tomodachi	[toh•moh•da´chee]	=	friend